Rowing Strength & Conditioning Log

This Book Belongs To:

_____

Visit http://elegantnotebooks.com for more sports training books.

Training Log and Diary
Nutrition Log and Diary
Strength and Conditioning Log and Diary

©Elegant Notebooks

DATE:	WEEK:	WEIGHT:

Warm Up/ Stretching **Duration:**

Exercise		Set 1	Set 2	Set 3	Set 4	Set 5
	Weight					
	Reps					
	Weight					
	Reps					
	Weight					
	Reps					
	Weight					
	Reps					
	Weight					
	Reps					
	Weight					
	Reps					
	Weight					
	Reps					
	Weight					
	Reps					
	Weight					
	Reps					
	Weight					
	Reps					
	Weight					
	Reps					
	Weight					
	Reps					
	Weight					
	Reps					

CARDIO WORKOUT

Exercise	Duration	Pace	Heart Rate	Calories

WATER   1 cup per circle
(1 cup = 8 ounces ~ 240ml)   ○○○○○○○○○○○○○○

DATE:		WEEK:		WEIGHT:	

Warm Up/ Stretching

Duration:

Exercise		Set 1	Set 2	Set 3	Set 4	Set 5
	Weight					
	Reps					
	Weight					
	Reps					
	Weight					
	Reps					
	Weight					
	Reps					
	Weight					
	Reps					
	Weight					
	Reps					
	Weight					
	Reps					
	Weight					
	Reps					
	Weight					
	Reps					
	Weight					
	Reps					
	Weight					
	Reps					
	Weight					
	Reps					

CARDIO WORKOUT

Exercise	Duration	Pace	Heart Rate	Calories

WATER 1 cup per circle
(1 cup = 8 ounces ~ 240ml)

○○○○○○○○○○○○○○○

DATE:	WEEK:	WEIGHT:

Warm Up/ Stretching

Duration:

Exercise		Set 1	Set 2	Set 3	Set 4	Set 5
	Weight					
	Reps					
	Weight					
	Reps					
	Weight					
	Reps					
	Weight					
	Reps					
	Weight					
	Reps					
	Weight					
	Reps					
	Weight					
	Reps					
	Weight					
	Reps					
	Weight					
	Reps					
	Weight					
	Reps					
	Weight					
	Reps					
	Weight					
	Reps					
	Weight					
	Reps					

CARDIO WORKOUT

Exercise	Duration	Pace	Heart Rate	Calories

WATER   1 cup per circle
(1 cup = 8 ounces ~ 240ml)

○ ○ ○ ○ ○ ○ ○ ○ ○ ○ ○ ○ ○

DATE: **WEEK:** **WEIGHT:**

Warm Up/ Stretching **Duration:**

Exercise		Set 1	Set 2	Set 3	Set 4	Set 5
	Weight					
	Reps					
	Weight					
	Reps					
	Weight					
	Reps					
	Weight					
	Reps					
	Weight					
	Reps					
	Weight					
	Reps					
	Weight					
	Reps					
	Weight					
	Reps					
	Weight					
	Reps					
	Weight					
	Reps					
	Weight					
	Reps					
	Weight					
	Reps					

CARDIO WORKOUT

Exercise	Duration	Pace	Heart Rate	Calories

WATER 1 cup per circle
(1 cup = 8 ounces ~ 240ml)   ○○○○○○○○○○○○○○○○

DATE:		WEEK:		WEIGHT:	

Warm Up/ Stretching

Duration:

Exercise		Set 1	Set 2	Set 3	Set 4	Set 5
	Weight					
	Reps					
	Weight					
	Reps					
	Weight					
	Reps					
	Weight					
	Reps					
	Weight					
	Reps					
	Weight					
	Reps					
	Weight					
	Reps					
	Weight					
	Reps					
	Weight					
	Reps					
	Weight					
	Reps					
	Weight					
	Reps					
	Weight					
	Reps					

CARDIO WORKOUT

Exercise	Duration	Pace	Heart Rate	Calories

WATER 1 cup per circle
(1 cup = 8 ounces ~ 240ml)

○○○○○○○○○○○○○○○

DATE:	WEEK:	WEIGHT:

Warm Up/ Stretching					Duration:	

Exercise		Set 1	Set 2	Set 3	Set 4	Set 5
	Weight					
	Reps					
	Weight					
	Reps					
	Weight					
	Reps					
	Weight					
	Reps					
	Weight					
	Reps					
	Weight					
	Reps					
	Weight					
	Reps					
	Weight					
	Reps					
	Weight					
	Reps					
	Weight					
	Reps					
	Weight					
	Reps					
	Weight					
	Reps					

CARDIO WORKOUT

Exercise	Duration	Pace	Heart Rate	Calories

WATER 1 cup per circle
(1 cup = 8 ounces ~ 240ml)

○○○○○○○○○○○○○○○○

DATE: _____ **WEEK:** ___ **WEIGHT:** _____

Warm Up/ Stretching					**Duration:** ___

Exercise		Set 1	Set 2	Set 3	Set 4	Set 5
	Weight					
	Reps					
	Weight					
	Reps					
	Weight					
	Reps					
	Weight					
	Reps					
	Weight					
	Reps					
	Weight					
	Reps					
	Weight					
	Reps					
	Weight					
	Reps					
	Weight					
	Reps					
	Weight					
	Reps					
	Weight					
	Reps					
	Weight					
	Reps					

CARDIO WORKOUT

Exercise	Duration	Pace	Heart Rate	Calories

WATER 1 cup per circle
(1 cup = 8 ounces ~ 240ml)   ○○○○○○○○○○○○○○

DATE:	WEEK:	WEIGHT:

Warm Up/ Stretching

Duration:

Exercise		Set 1	Set 2	Set 3	Set 4	Set 5
	Weight					
	Reps					
	Weight					
	Reps					
	Weight					
	Reps					
	Weight					
	Reps					
	Weight					
	Reps					
	Weight					
	Reps					
	Weight					
	Reps					
	Weight					
	Reps					
	Weight					
	Reps					
	Weight					
	Reps					
	Weight					
	Reps					
	Weight					
	Reps					

CARDIO WORKOUT

Exercise	Duration	Pace	Heart Rate	Calories

WATER 1 cup per circle
(1 cup = 8 ounces ~ 240ml)

○○○○○○○○○○○○○○○○

DATE:	WEEK:	WEIGHT:

Warm Up/ Stretching

Duration:

Exercise		Set 1	Set 2	Set 3	Set 4	Set 5
	Weight					
	Reps					
	Weight					
	Reps					
	Weight					
	Reps					
	Weight					
	Reps					
	Weight					
	Reps					
	Weight					
	Reps					
	Weight					
	Reps					
	Weight					
	Reps					
	Weight					
	Reps					
	Weight					
	Reps					
	Weight					
	Reps					
	Weight					
	Reps					
	Weight					
	Reps					

CARDIO WORKOUT

Exercise	Duration	Pace	Heart Rate	Calories

WATER 1 cup per circle
(1 cup = 8 ounces ~ 240ml)

○○○○○○○○○○○○○○

| DATE: | | WEEK: | | WEIGHT: | |

Warm Up/ Stretching

Duration:

Exercise		Set 1	Set 2	Set 3	Set 4	Set 5
	Weight					
	Reps					
	Weight					
	Reps					
	Weight					
	Reps					
	Weight					
	Reps					
	Weight					
	Reps					
	Weight					
	Reps					
	Weight					
	Reps					
	Weight					
	Reps					
	Weight					
	Reps					
	Weight					
	Reps					
	Weight					
	Reps					
	Weight					
	Reps					
	Weight					
	Reps					

CARDIO WORKOUT

Exercise	Duration	Pace	Heart Rate	Calories

WATER 1 cup per circle
(1 cup = 8 ounces ~ 240ml)

○○○○○○○○○○○○○○○○

| DATE: | WEEK: | WEIGHT: |

| Warm Up/ Stretching | | | | Duration: | |

Exercise		Set 1	Set 2	Set 3	Set 4	Set 5
	Weight					
	Reps					
	Weight					
	Reps					
	Weight					
	Reps					
	Weight					
	Reps					
	Weight					
	Reps					
	Weight					
	Reps					
	Weight					
	Reps					
	Weight					
	Reps					
	Weight					
	Reps					
	Weight					
	Reps					
	Weight					
	Reps					
	Weight					
	Reps					

CARDIO WORKOUT

Exercise	Duration	Pace	Heart Rate	Calories

WATER 1 cup per circle
(1 cup = 8 ounces ~ 240ml)   ○○○○○○○○○○○○○○○○

DATE:	WEEK:	WEIGHT:

Warm Up/ Stretching

Duration:

Exercise		Set 1	Set 2	Set 3	Set 4	Set 5
	Weight					
	Reps					
	Weight					
	Reps					
	Weight					
	Reps					
	Weight					
	Reps					
	Weight					
	Reps					
	Weight					
	Reps					
	Weight					
	Reps					
	Weight					
	Reps					
	Weight					
	Reps					
	Weight					
	Reps					
	Weight					
	Reps					
	Weight					
	Reps					
	Weight					
	Reps					

CARDIO WORKOUT

Exercise	Duration	Pace	Heart Rate	Calories

WATER 1 cup per circle
(1 cup = 8 ounces ~ 240ml)

○○○○○○○○○○○○○○○

DATE:	WEEK:	WEIGHT:

Warm Up/ Stretching		Duration:

Exercise		Set 1	Set 2	Set 3	Set 4	Set 5
	Weight					
	Reps					
	Weight					
	Reps					
	Weight					
	Reps					
	Weight					
	Reps					
	Weight					
	Reps					
	Weight					
	Reps					
	Weight					
	Reps					
	Weight					
	Reps					
	Weight					
	Reps					
	Weight					
	Reps					
	Weight					
	Reps					
	Weight					
	Reps					

CARDIO WORKOUT

Exercise	Duration	Pace	Heart Rate	Calories

WATER 1 cup per circle
(1 cup = 8 ounces ~ 240ml)   ○○○○○○○○○○○○○○

DATE:	WEEK:	WEIGHT:

Warm Up/ Stretching		Duration:

Exercise		Set 1	Set 2	Set 3	Set 4	Set 5
	Weight					
	Reps					
	Weight					
	Reps					
	Weight					
	Reps					
	Weight					
	Reps					
	Weight					
	Reps					
	Weight					
	Reps					
	Weight					
	Reps					
	Weight					
	Reps					
	Weight					
	Reps					
	Weight					
	Reps					
	Weight					
	Reps					
	Weight					
	Reps					
	Weight					
	Reps					

CARDIO WORKOUT

Exercise	Duration	Pace	Heart Rate	Calories

WATER 1 cup per circle
(1 cup = 8 ounces ~ 240ml)

○ ○ ○ ○ ○ ○ ○ ○ ○ ○ ○ ○ ○ ○ ○

DATE:	WEEK:	WEIGHT:

Warm Up/ Stretching   **Duration:**

Exercise		Set 1	Set 2	Set 3	Set 4	Set 5
	Weight					
	Reps					
	Weight					
	Reps					
	Weight					
	Reps					
	Weight					
	Reps					
	Weight					
	Reps					
	Weight					
	Reps					
	Weight					
	Reps					
	Weight					
	Reps					
	Weight					
	Reps					
	Weight					
	Reps					
	Weight					
	Reps					
	Weight					
	Reps					
	Weight					
	Reps					

CARDIO WORKOUT

Exercise	Duration	Pace	Heart Rate	Calories

WATER   1 cup per circle
(1 cup = 8 ounces ~ 240ml)   ○○○○○○○○○○○○○○

| DATE: | | WEEK: | | WEIGHT: | |

| Warm Up/ Stretching | | | | | Duration: | |

Exercise		Set 1	Set 2	Set 3	Set 4	Set 5
	Weight					
	Reps					
	Weight					
	Reps					
	Weight					
	Reps					
	Weight					
	Reps					
	Weight					
	Reps					
	Weight					
	Reps					
	Weight					
	Reps					
	Weight					
	Reps					
	Weight					
	Reps					
	Weight					
	Reps					
	Weight					
	Reps					
	Weight					
	Reps					
	Weight					
	Reps					

CARDIO WORKOUT

Exercise	Duration	Pace	Heart Rate	Calories

WATER   1 cup per circle
(1 cup = 8 ounces ~ 240ml)   ○ ○ ○ ○ ○ ○ ○ ○ ○ ○ ○ ○ ○ ○

DATE:	WEEK:	WEIGHT:

Warm Up/ Stretching — Duration:

Exercise		Set 1	Set 2	Set 3	Set 4	Set 5
	Weight					
	Reps					
	Weight					
	Reps					
	Weight					
	Reps					
	Weight					
	Reps					
	Weight					
	Reps					
	Weight					
	Reps					
	Weight					
	Reps					
	Weight					
	Reps					
	Weight					
	Reps					
	Weight					
	Reps					
	Weight					
	Reps					
	Weight					
	Reps					
	Weight					
	Reps					

CARDIO WORKOUT

Exercise	Duration	Pace	Heart Rate	Calories

WATER 1 cup per circle
(1 cup = 8 ounces ~ 240ml)   ○○○○○○○○○○○○○○○

DATE:		WEEK:		WEIGHT:	

Warm Up/ Stretching				Duration:	

Exercise		Set 1	Set 2	Set 3	Set 4	Set 5
	Weight					
	Reps					
	Weight					
	Reps					
	Weight					
	Reps					
	Weight					
	Reps					
	Weight					
	Reps					
	Weight					
	Reps					
	Weight					
	Reps					
	Weight					
	Reps					
	Weight					
	Reps					
	Weight					
	Reps					
	Weight					
	Reps					
	Weight					
	Reps					
	Weight					
	Reps					

CARDIO WORKOUT

Exercise	Duration	Pace	Heart Rate	Calories

WATER   1 cup per circle
(1 cup = 8 ounces ~ 240ml)   ○○○○○○○○○○○○○○○

DATE:		WEEK:		WEIGHT:	

Warm Up/ Stretching				Duration:	

Exercise		Set 1	Set 2	Set 3	Set 4	Set 5
	Weight					
	Reps					
	Weight					
	Reps					
	Weight					
	Reps					
	Weight					
	Reps					
	Weight					
	Reps					
	Weight					
	Reps					
	Weight					
	Reps					
	Weight					
	Reps					
	Weight					
	Reps					
	Weight					
	Reps					
	Weight					
	Reps					
	Weight					
	Reps					

CARDIO WORKOUT

Exercise	Duration	Pace	Heart Rate	Calories

WATER 1 cup per circle
(1 cup = 8 ounces ~ 240ml)   ○○○○○○○○○○○○○○○○

DATE:		WEEK:		WEIGHT:	

Warm Up/ Stretching				Duration:	

Exercise		Set 1	Set 2	Set 3	Set 4	Set 5
	Weight					
	Reps					
	Weight					
	Reps					
	Weight					
	Reps					
	Weight					
	Reps					
	Weight					
	Reps					
	Weight					
	Reps					
	Weight					
	Reps					
	Weight					
	Reps					
	Weight					
	Reps					
	Weight					
	Reps					
	Weight					
	Reps					
	Weight					
	Reps					
	Weight					
	Reps					

CARDIO WORKOUT

Exercise	Duration	Pace	Heart Rate	Calories

WATER 1 cup per circle
(1 cup = 8 ounces ~ 240ml)   ○○○○○○○○○○○○○○

| DATE: | | WEEK: | | WEIGHT: | |

Warm Up/ Stretching

Duration:

Exercise		Set 1	Set 2	Set 3	Set 4	Set 5
	Weight					
	Reps					
	Weight					
	Reps					
	Weight					
	Reps					
	Weight					
	Reps					
	Weight					
	Reps					
	Weight					
	Reps					
	Weight					
	Reps					
	Weight					
	Reps					
	Weight					
	Reps					
	Weight					
	Reps					
	Weight					
	Reps					
	Weight					
	Reps					
	Weight					
	Reps					

CARDIO WORKOUT

Exercise	Duration	Pace	Heart Rate	Calories

WATER 1 cup per circle
(1 cup = 8 ounces ~ 240ml)   ○○○○○○○○○○○○○○

DATE: **WEEK:**   **WEIGHT:**

Warm Up/ Stretching   **Duration:**

Exercise		Set 1	Set 2	Set 3	Set 4	Set 5
	Weight					
	Reps					
	Weight					
	Reps					
	Weight					
	Reps					
	Weight					
	Reps					
	Weight					
	Reps					
	Weight					
	Reps					
	Weight					
	Reps					
	Weight					
	Reps					
	Weight					
	Reps					
	Weight					
	Reps					
	Weight					
	Reps					
	Weight					
	Reps					

CARDIO WORKOUT

Exercise	Duration	Pace	Heart Rate	Calories

WATER   1 cup per circle
(1 cup = 8 ounces ~ 240ml)   ○○○○○○○○○○○○○○○○

DATE: | **WEEK:** | **WEIGHT:**

| Warm Up/ Stretching | | | | | **Duration:** | |

Exercise		Set 1	Set 2	Set 3	Set 4	Set 5
	Weight					
	Reps					
	Weight					
	Reps					
	Weight					
	Reps					
	Weight					
	Reps					
	Weight					
	Reps					
	Weight					
	Reps					
	Weight					
	Reps					
	Weight					
	Reps					
	Weight					
	Reps					
	Weight					
	Reps					
	Weight					
	Reps					
	Weight					
	Reps					
	Weight					
	Reps					

CARDIO WORKOUT

Exercise	Duration	Pace	Heart Rate	Calories

WATER 1 cup per circle
(1 cup = 8 ounces ~ 240ml)   ○○○○○○○○○○○○○○○

DATE:	WEEK:	WEIGHT:

Warm Up/ Stretching		Duration:

Exercise		Set 1	Set 2	Set 3	Set 4	Set 5
	Weight					
	Reps					
	Weight					
	Reps					
	Weight					
	Reps					
	Weight					
	Reps					
	Weight					
	Reps					
	Weight					
	Reps					
	Weight					
	Reps					
	Weight					
	Reps					
	Weight					
	Reps					
	Weight					
	Reps					
	Weight					
	Reps					
	Weight					
	Reps					
	Weight					
	Reps					

CARDIO WORKOUT

Exercise	Duration	Pace	Heart Rate	Calories

WATER 1 cup per circle
(1 cup = 8 ounces ~ 240ml) ○○○○○○○○○○○○○○○○

DATE:		WEEK:		WEIGHT:	

Warm Up/ Stretching				Duration:	

Exercise		Set 1	Set 2	Set 3	Set 4	Set 5
	Weight					
	Reps					
	Weight					
	Reps					
	Weight					
	Reps					
	Weight					
	Reps					
	Weight					
	Reps					
	Weight					
	Reps					
	Weight					
	Reps					
	Weight					
	Reps					
	Weight					
	Reps					
	Weight					
	Reps					
	Weight					
	Reps					
	Weight					
	Reps					

CARDIO WORKOUT

Exercise	Duration	Pace	Heart Rate	Calories

WATER 1 cup per circle
(1 cup = 8 ounces ~ 240ml)   ○○○○○○○○○○○○○○

DATE:		WEEK:		WEIGHT:	

Warm Up/ Stretching				Duration:	

Exercise		Set 1	Set 2	Set 3	Set 4	Set 5
	Weight					
	Reps					
	Weight					
	Reps					
	Weight					
	Reps					
	Weight					
	Reps					
	Weight					
	Reps					
	Weight					
	Reps					
	Weight					
	Reps					
	Weight					
	Reps					
	Weight					
	Reps					
	Weight					
	Reps					
	Weight					
	Reps					
	Weight					
	Reps					
	Weight					
	Reps					

CARDIO WORKOUT

Exercise	Duration	Pace	Heart Rate	Calories

WATER 1 cup per circle
(1 cup = 8 ounces ~ 240ml)   ◯ ◯ ◯ ◯ ◯ ◯ ◯ ◯ ◯ ◯ ◯ ◯ ◯ ◯ ◯

| DATE: | | WEEK: | | WEIGHT: | |

Warm Up/ Stretching

Duration:

Exercise		Set 1	Set 2	Set 3	Set 4	Set 5
	Weight					
	Reps					
	Weight					
	Reps					
	Weight					
	Reps					
	Weight					
	Reps					
	Weight					
	Reps					
	Weight					
	Reps					
	Weight					
	Reps					
	Weight					
	Reps					
	Weight					
	Reps					
	Weight					
	Reps					
	Weight					
	Reps					
	Weight					
	Reps					

CARDIO WORKOUT

Exercise	Duration	Pace	Heart Rate	Calories

WATER 1 cup per circle
(1 cup = 8 ounces ~ 240ml)

○○○○○○○○○○○○○○○○

DATE:		WEEK:		WEIGHT:	

Warm Up/ Stretching			Duration:	

Exercise		Set 1	Set 2	Set 3	Set 4	Set 5
	Weight					
	Reps					
	Weight					
	Reps					
	Weight					
	Reps					
	Weight					
	Reps					
	Weight					
	Reps					
	Weight					
	Reps					
	Weight					
	Reps					
	Weight					
	Reps					
	Weight					
	Reps					
	Weight					
	Reps					
	Weight					
	Reps					
	Weight					
	Reps					
	Weight					
	Reps					

CARDIO WORKOUT

Exercise	Duration	Pace	Heart Rate	Calories

WATER 1 cup per circle
(1 cup = 8 ounces ~ 240ml)   ○○○○○○○○○○○○○○○

DATE: _____   **WEEK:** _____   **WEIGHT:** _____

Warm Up/ Stretching

Duration: _____

Exercise		Set 1	Set 2	Set 3	Set 4	Set 5
	Weight					
	Reps					
	Weight					
	Reps					
	Weight					
	Reps					
	Weight					
	Reps					
	Weight					
	Reps					
	Weight					
	Reps					
	Weight					
	Reps					
	Weight					
	Reps					
	Weight					
	Reps					
	Weight					
	Reps					
	Weight					
	Reps					
	Weight					
	Reps					

CARDIO WORKOUT

Exercise	Duration	Pace	Heart Rate	Calories

WATER   1 cup per circle
(1 cup = 8 ounces ~ 240ml)

○ ○ ○ ○ ○ ○ ○ ○ ○ ○ ○ ○ ○ ○

DATE:	WEEK:	WEIGHT:

Warm Up/ Stretching	Duration:

Exercise		Set 1	Set 2	Set 3	Set 4	Set 5
	Weight					
	Reps					
	Weight					
	Reps					
	Weight					
	Reps					
	Weight					
	Reps					
	Weight					
	Reps					
	Weight					
	Reps					
	Weight					
	Reps					
	Weight					
	Reps					
	Weight					
	Reps					
	Weight					
	Reps					
	Weight					
	Reps					
	Weight					
	Reps					

CARDIO WORKOUT

Exercise	Duration	Pace	Heart Rate	Calories

WATER 1 cup per circle
(1 cup = 8 ounces ~ 240ml)   ○○○○○○○○○○○○○○○

DATE:		WEEK:		WEIGHT:	

Warm Up/ Stretching				Duration:	

Exercise		Set 1	Set 2	Set 3	Set 4	Set 5
	Weight					
	Reps					
	Weight					
	Reps					
	Weight					
	Reps					
	Weight					
	Reps					
	Weight					
	Reps					
	Weight					
	Reps					
	Weight					
	Reps					
	Weight					
	Reps					
	Weight					
	Reps					
	Weight					
	Reps					
	Weight					
	Reps					
	Weight					
	Reps					

CARDIO WORKOUT

Exercise	Duration	Pace	Heart Rate	Calories

WATER 1 cup per circle
(1 cup = 8 ounces ~ 240ml)   ○○○○○○○○○○○○○○○

DATE:	WEEK:	WEIGHT:

Warm Up/ Stretching	Duration:

Exercise		Set 1	Set 2	Set 3	Set 4	Set 5
	Weight					
	Reps					
	Weight					
	Reps					
	Weight					
	Reps					
	Weight					
	Reps					
	Weight					
	Reps					
	Weight					
	Reps					
	Weight					
	Reps					
	Weight					
	Reps					
	Weight					
	Reps					
	Weight					
	Reps					
	Weight					
	Reps					
	Weight					
	Reps					
	Weight					
	Reps					

CARDIO WORKOUT

Exercise	Duration	Pace	Heart Rate	Calories

WATER 1 cup per circle
(1 cup = 8 ounces ~ 240ml)   ○○○○○○○○○○○○○○○

| DATE: | WEEK: | WEIGHT: |

Warm Up/ Stretching			Duration:		

Exercise		Set 1	Set 2	Set 3	Set 4	Set 5
	Weight					
	Reps					
	Weight					
	Reps					
	Weight					
	Reps					
	Weight					
	Reps					
	Weight					
	Reps					
	Weight					
	Reps					
	Weight					
	Reps					
	Weight					
	Reps					
	Weight					
	Reps					
	Weight					
	Reps					
	Weight					
	Reps					
	Weight					
	Reps					
	Weight					
	Reps					

CARDIO WORKOUT

Exercise	Duration	Pace	Heart Rate	Calories

WATER 1 cup per circle
(1 cup = 8 ounces ~ 240ml)   ○○○○○○○○○○○○○○○

DATE:	WEEK:	WEIGHT:

Warm Up/ Stretching

Duration:

Exercise		Set 1	Set 2	Set 3	Set 4	Set 5
	Weight					
	Reps					
	Weight					
	Reps					
	Weight					
	Reps					
	Weight					
	Reps					
	Weight					
	Reps					
	Weight					
	Reps					
	Weight					
	Reps					
	Weight					
	Reps					
	Weight					
	Reps					
	Weight					
	Reps					
	Weight					
	Reps					
	Weight					
	Reps					

CARDIO WORKOUT

Exercise	Duration	Pace	Heart Rate	Calories

WATER 1 cup per circle
(1 cup = 8 ounces ~ 240ml)

○ ○ ○ ○ ○ ○ ○ ○ ○ ○ ○ ○ ○ ○ ○ ○

DATE:	WEEK:	WEIGHT:

Warm Up/ Stretching				Duration:	

Exercise		Set 1	Set 2	Set 3	Set 4	Set 5
	Weight					
	Reps					
	Weight					
	Reps					
	Weight					
	Reps					
	Weight					
	Reps					
	Weight					
	Reps					
	Weight					
	Reps					
	Weight					
	Reps					
	Weight					
	Reps					
	Weight					
	Reps					
	Weight					
	Reps					
	Weight					
	Reps					
	Weight					
	Reps					

CARDIO WORKOUT

Exercise	Duration	Pace	Heart Rate	Calories

WATER 1 cup per circle
(1 cup = 8 ounces ~ 240ml)

○ ○ ○ ○ ○ ○ ○ ○ ○ ○ ○ ○ ○ ○

DATE:		WEEK:		WEIGHT:	

Warm Up/ Stretching				Duration:	

Exercise		Set 1	Set 2	Set 3	Set 4	Set 5
	Weight					
	Reps					
	Weight					
	Reps					
	Weight					
	Reps					
	Weight					
	Reps					
	Weight					
	Reps					
	Weight					
	Reps					
	Weight					
	Reps					
	Weight					
	Reps					
	Weight					
	Reps					
	Weight					
	Reps					
	Weight					
	Reps					
	Weight					
	Reps					

CARDIO WORKOUT

Exercise	Duration	Pace	Heart Rate	Calories

WATER 1 cup per circle
(1 cup = 8 ounces ~ 240ml)

○○○○○○○○○○○○○○○○

DATE:	WEEK:	WEIGHT:

Warm Up/ Stretching — Duration:

Exercise		Set 1	Set 2	Set 3	Set 4	Set 5
	Weight					
	Reps					
	Weight					
	Reps					
	Weight					
	Reps					
	Weight					
	Reps					
	Weight					
	Reps					
	Weight					
	Reps					
	Weight					
	Reps					
	Weight					
	Reps					
	Weight					
	Reps					
	Weight					
	Reps					
	Weight					
	Reps					
	Weight					
	Reps					
	Weight					
	Reps					

CARDIO WORKOUT

Exercise	Duration	Pace	Heart Rate	Calories

WATER 1 cup per circle
(1 cup = 8 ounces ~ 240ml)   ○○○○○○○○○○○○○○○

DATE:		WEEK:		WEIGHT:	

Warm Up/ Stretching				Duration:	

Exercise		Set 1	Set 2	Set 3	Set 4	Set 5
	Weight					
	Reps					
	Weight					
	Reps					
	Weight					
	Reps					
	Weight					
	Reps					
	Weight					
	Reps					
	Weight					
	Reps					
	Weight					
	Reps					
	Weight					
	Reps					
	Weight					
	Reps					
	Weight					
	Reps					
	Weight					
	Reps					
	Weight					
	Reps					
	Weight					
	Reps					

CARDIO WORKOUT

Exercise	Duration	Pace	Heart Rate	Calories

WATER   1 cup per circle
(1 cup = 8 ounces ~ 240ml)   ○○○○○○○○○○○○○○○

DATE: _____   **WEEK:** _____   **WEIGHT:** _____

| Warm Up/ Stretching | | | | | Duration: | |

Exercise		Set 1	Set 2	Set 3	Set 4	Set 5
	Weight					
	Reps					
	Weight					
	Reps					
	Weight					
	Reps					
	Weight					
	Reps					
	Weight					
	Reps					
	Weight					
	Reps					
	Weight					
	Reps					
	Weight					
	Reps					
	Weight					
	Reps					
	Weight					
	Reps					
	Weight					
	Reps					
	Weight					
	Reps					
	Weight					
	Reps					

CARDIO WORKOUT

Exercise	Duration	Pace	Heart Rate	Calories

WATER 1 cup per circle
(1 cup = 8 ounces ~ 240ml)   ○○○○○○○○○○○○○○○

DATE:	WEEK:	WEIGHT:

Warm Up/ Stretching		Duration:	

Exercise		Set 1	Set 2	Set 3	Set 4	Set 5
	Weight					
	Reps					
	Weight					
	Reps					
	Weight					
	Reps					
	Weight					
	Reps					
	Weight					
	Reps					
	Weight					
	Reps					
	Weight					
	Reps					
	Weight					
	Reps					
	Weight					
	Reps					
	Weight					
	Reps					
	Weight					
	Reps					
	Weight					
	Reps					
	Weight					
	Reps					

CARDIO WORKOUT

Exercise	Duration	Pace	Heart Rate	Calories

WATER 1 cup per circle
(1 cup = 8 ounces ~ 240ml)   ○○○○○○○○○○○○○○○

DATE:	WEEK:	WEIGHT:

Warm Up/ Stretching

Duration:

Exercise		Set 1	Set 2	Set 3	Set 4	Set 5
	Weight					
	Reps					
	Weight					
	Reps					
	Weight					
	Reps					
	Weight					
	Reps					
	Weight					
	Reps					
	Weight					
	Reps					
	Weight					
	Reps					
	Weight					
	Reps					
	Weight					
	Reps					
	Weight					
	Reps					
	Weight					
	Reps					
	Weight					
	Reps					
	Weight					
	Reps					

CARDIO WORKOUT

Exercise	Duration	Pace	Heart Rate	Calories

WATER 1 cup per circle
(1 cup = 8 ounces ~ 240ml)   ○○○○○○○○○○○○○○○○○○

DATE: **WEEK:**   **WEIGHT:**

Warm Up/ Stretching   **Duration:**

Exercise		Set 1	Set 2	Set 3	Set 4	Set 5
	Weight					
	Reps					
	Weight					
	Reps					
	Weight					
	Reps					
	Weight					
	Reps					
	Weight					
	Reps					
	Weight					
	Reps					
	Weight					
	Reps					
	Weight					
	Reps					
	Weight					
	Reps					
	Weight					
	Reps					
	Weight					
	Reps					
	Weight					
	Reps					

CARDIO WORKOUT

Exercise	Duration	Pace	Heart Rate	Calories

WATER   1 cup per circle
(1 cup = 8 ounces ~ 240ml)   ○○○○○○○○○○○○○○○○

DATE: [ ] WEEK: [ ] WEIGHT: [ ]

Warm Up/ Stretching   Duration: [ ]

Exercise		Set 1	Set 2	Set 3	Set 4	Set 5
	Weight					
	Reps					
	Weight					
	Reps					
	Weight					
	Reps					
	Weight					
	Reps					
	Weight					
	Reps					
	Weight					
	Reps					
	Weight					
	Reps					
	Weight					
	Reps					
	Weight					
	Reps					
	Weight					
	Reps					
	Weight					
	Reps					
	Weight					
	Reps					
	Weight					
	Reps					

CARDIO WORKOUT

Exercise	Duration	Pace	Heart Rate	Calories

WATER 1 cup per circle
(1 cup = 8 ounces ~ 240ml)   ○○○○○○○○○○○○○○○

DATE:	WEEK:	WEIGHT:

Warm Up/ Stretching		Duration:

Exercise		Set 1	Set 2	Set 3	Set 4	Set 5
	Weight					
	Reps					
	Weight					
	Reps					
	Weight					
	Reps					
	Weight					
	Reps					
	Weight					
	Reps					
	Weight					
	Reps					
	Weight					
	Reps					
	Weight					
	Reps					
	Weight					
	Reps					
	Weight					
	Reps					
	Weight					
	Reps					
	Weight					
	Reps					

CARDIO WORKOUT

Exercise	Duration	Pace	Heart Rate	Calories

WATER 1 cup per circle
(1 cup = 8 ounces ~ 240ml)

○ ○ ○ ○ ○ ○ ○ ○ ○ ○ ○ ○ ○ ○ ○ ○

DATE:		WEEK:		WEIGHT:	

Warm Up/ Stretching

Duration:

Exercise		Set 1	Set 2	Set 3	Set 4	Set 5
	Weight					
	Reps					
	Weight					
	Reps					
	Weight					
	Reps					
	Weight					
	Reps					
	Weight					
	Reps					
	Weight					
	Reps					
	Weight					
	Reps					
	Weight					
	Reps					
	Weight					
	Reps					
	Weight					
	Reps					
	Weight					
	Reps					
	Weight					
	Reps					
	Weight					
	Reps					

CARDIO WORKOUT

Exercise	Duration	Pace	Heart Rate	Calories

WATER 1 cup per circle
(1 cup = 8 ounces ~ 240ml)

○○○○○○○○○○○○○○○○

DATE:	WEEK:	WEIGHT:

Warm Up/ Stretching	Duration:

Exercise		Set 1	Set 2	Set 3	Set 4	Set 5
	Weight					
	Reps					
	Weight					
	Reps					
	Weight					
	Reps					
	Weight					
	Reps					
	Weight					
	Reps					
	Weight					
	Reps					
	Weight					
	Reps					
	Weight					
	Reps					
	Weight					
	Reps					
	Weight					
	Reps					
	Weight					
	Reps					
	Weight					
	Reps					

CARDIO WORKOUT

Exercise	Duration	Pace	Heart Rate	Calories

WATER 1 cup per circle
(1 cup = 8 ounces ~ 240ml)

○○○○○○○○○○○○○○○○

DATE:	WEEK:	WEIGHT:

Warm Up/ Stretching

Duration:

Exercise		Set 1	Set 2	Set 3	Set 4	Set 5
	Weight					
	Reps					
	Weight					
	Reps					
	Weight					
	Reps					
	Weight					
	Reps					
	Weight					
	Reps					
	Weight					
	Reps					
	Weight					
	Reps					
	Weight					
	Reps					
	Weight					
	Reps					
	Weight					
	Reps					
	Weight					
	Reps					
	Weight					
	Reps					

CARDIO WORKOUT

Exercise	Duration	Pace	Heart Rate	Calories

WATER 1 cup per circle
(1 cup = 8 ounces ~ 240ml)

○○○○○○○○○○○○○○○○

DATE:		WEEK:		WEIGHT:	

Warm Up/ Stretching				Duration:	

Exercise		Set 1	Set 2	Set 3	Set 4	Set 5
	Weight					
	Reps					
	Weight					
	Reps					
	Weight					
	Reps					
	Weight					
	Reps					
	Weight					
	Reps					
	Weight					
	Reps					
	Weight					
	Reps					
	Weight					
	Reps					
	Weight					
	Reps					
	Weight					
	Reps					
	Weight					
	Reps					
	Weight					
	Reps					
	Weight					
	Reps					

CARDIO WORKOUT

Exercise	Duration	Pace	Heart Rate	Calories

WATER   1 cup per circle
(1 cup = 8 ounces ~ 240ml)   ○○○○○○○○○○○○○○○○

DATE:		WEEK:		WEIGHT:	

Warm Up/ Stretching			Duration:	

Exercise		Set 1	Set 2	Set 3	Set 4	Set 5
	Weight					
	Reps					
	Weight					
	Reps					
	Weight					
	Reps					
	Weight					
	Reps					
	Weight					
	Reps					
	Weight					
	Reps					
	Weight					
	Reps					
	Weight					
	Reps					
	Weight					
	Reps					
	Weight					
	Reps					
	Weight					
	Reps					
	Weight					
	Reps					
	Weight					
	Reps					

CARDIO WORKOUT

Exercise	Duration	Pace	Heart Rate	Calories

WATER 1 cup per circle
(1 cup = 8 ounces ~ 240ml)   ○○○○○○○○○○○○○○○○

DATE:	WEEK:	WEIGHT:

Warm Up/ Stretching				Duration:		

Exercise		Set 1	Set 2	Set 3	Set 4	Set 5
	Weight					
	Reps					
	Weight					
	Reps					
	Weight					
	Reps					
	Weight					
	Reps					
	Weight					
	Reps					
	Weight					
	Reps					
	Weight					
	Reps					
	Weight					
	Reps					
	Weight					
	Reps					
	Weight					
	Reps					
	Weight					
	Reps					
	Weight					
	Reps					
	Weight					
	Reps					

CARDIO WORKOUT

Exercise	Duration	Pace	Heart Rate	Calories

WATER 1 cup per circle
(1 cup = 8 ounces ~ 240ml)   ○○○○○○○○○○○○○○○○

DATE:		WEEK:		WEIGHT:	

Warm Up/ Stretching				Duration:	

Exercise		Set 1	Set 2	Set 3	Set 4	Set 5
	Weight					
	Reps					
	Weight					
	Reps					
	Weight					
	Reps					
	Weight					
	Reps					
	Weight					
	Reps					
	Weight					
	Reps					
	Weight					
	Reps					
	Weight					
	Reps					
	Weight					
	Reps					
	Weight					
	Reps					
	Weight					
	Reps					
	Weight					
	Reps					
	Weight					
	Reps					

CARDIO WORKOUT

Exercise	Duration	Pace	Heart Rate	Calories

WATER 1 cup per circle
(1 cup = 8 ounces ~ 240ml)   ○○○○○○○○○○○○○○○○

DATE:		WEEK:	WEIGHT:	

Warm Up/ Stretching				Duration:	

Exercise		Set 1	Set 2	Set 3	Set 4	Set 5
	Weight					
	Reps					
	Weight					
	Reps					
	Weight					
	Reps					
	Weight					
	Reps					
	Weight					
	Reps					
	Weight					
	Reps					
	Weight					
	Reps					
	Weight					
	Reps					
	Weight					
	Reps					
	Weight					
	Reps					
	Weight					
	Reps					
	Weight					
	Reps					
	Weight					
	Reps					

CARDIO WORKOUT

Exercise	Duration	Pace	Heart Rate	Calories

WATER 1 cup per circle
(1 cup = 8 ounces ~ 240ml)

○○○○○○○○○○○○○○○○

DATE:		WEEK:		WEIGHT:	

Warm Up/ Stretching				Duration:	

Exercise		Set 1	Set 2	Set 3	Set 4	Set 5
	Weight					
	Reps					
	Weight					
	Reps					
	Weight					
	Reps					
	Weight					
	Reps					
	Weight					
	Reps					
	Weight					
	Reps					
	Weight					
	Reps					
	Weight					
	Reps					
	Weight					
	Reps					
	Weight					
	Reps					
	Weight					
	Reps					
	Weight					
	Reps					
	Weight					
	Reps					

CARDIO WORKOUT

Exercise	Duration	Pace	Heart Rate	Calories

WATER 1 cup per circle
(1 cup = 8 ounces ~ 240ml)   ○○○○○○○○○○○○○○○○

DATE:	WEEK:	WEIGHT:

Warm Up/ Stretching				Duration:	

Exercise		Set 1	Set 2	Set 3	Set 4	Set 5
	Weight					
	Reps					
	Weight					
	Reps					
	Weight					
	Reps					
	Weight					
	Reps					
	Weight					
	Reps					
	Weight					
	Reps					
	Weight					
	Reps					
	Weight					
	Reps					
	Weight					
	Reps					
	Weight					
	Reps					
	Weight					
	Reps					
	Weight					
	Reps					
	Weight					
	Reps					

CARDIO WORKOUT

Exercise	Duration	Pace	Heart Rate	Calories

WATER   1 cup per circle
(1 cup = 8 ounces ~ 240ml)   ○○○○○○○○○○○○○○○○

DATE: **WEEK:** **WEIGHT:**

Warm Up/ Stretching **Duration:**

Exercise		Set 1	Set 2	Set 3	Set 4	Set 5
	Weight					
	Reps					
	Weight					
	Reps					
	Weight					
	Reps					
	Weight					
	Reps					
	Weight					
	Reps					
	Weight					
	Reps					
	Weight					
	Reps					
	Weight					
	Reps					
	Weight					
	Reps					
	Weight					
	Reps					
	Weight					
	Reps					
	Weight					
	Reps					

CARDIO WORKOUT

Exercise	Duration	Pace	Heart Rate	Calories

WATER 1 cup per circle
(1 cup = 8 ounces ~ 240ml)   ○○○○○○○○○○○○○○○○

DATE:	WEEK:	WEIGHT:

Warm Up/ Stretching

Duration:

Exercise		Set 1	Set 2	Set 3	Set 4	Set 5
	Weight					
	Reps					
	Weight					
	Reps					
	Weight					
	Reps					
	Weight					
	Reps					
	Weight					
	Reps					
	Weight					
	Reps					
	Weight					
	Reps					
	Weight					
	Reps					
	Weight					
	Reps					
	Weight					
	Reps					
	Weight					
	Reps					
	Weight					
	Reps					

CARDIO WORKOUT

Exercise	Duration	Pace	Heart Rate	Calories

WATER   1 cup per circle
(1 cup = 8 ounces ~ 240ml)

○○○○○○○○○○○○○○○

DATE:	WEEK:	WEIGHT:

Warm Up/ Stretching					Duration:	

Exercise		Set 1	Set 2	Set 3	Set 4	Set 5
	Weight					
	Reps					
	Weight					
	Reps					
	Weight					
	Reps					
	Weight					
	Reps					
	Weight					
	Reps					
	Weight					
	Reps					
	Weight					
	Reps					
	Weight					
	Reps					
	Weight					
	Reps					
	Weight					
	Reps					
	Weight					
	Reps					
	Weight					
	Reps					

CARDIO WORKOUT

Exercise	Duration	Pace	Heart Rate	Calories

WATER 1 cup per circle
(1 cup = 8 ounces ~ 240ml)   ○○○○○○○○○○○○○○○○

DATE:	WEEK:	WEIGHT:

Warm Up/ Stretching		Duration:

Exercise		Set 1	Set 2	Set 3	Set 4	Set 5
	Weight					
	Reps					
	Weight					
	Reps					
	Weight					
	Reps					
	Weight					
	Reps					
	Weight					
	Reps					
	Weight					
	Reps					
	Weight					
	Reps					
	Weight					
	Reps					
	Weight					
	Reps					
	Weight					
	Reps					
	Weight					
	Reps					
	Weight					
	Reps					
	Weight					
	Reps					

CARDIO WORKOUT

Exercise	Duration	Pace	Heart Rate	Calories

WATER 1 cup per circle
(1 cup = 8 ounces ~ 240ml)   ○○○○○○○○○○○○○○○

DATE:	WEEK:	WEIGHT:

Warm Up/ Stretching		Duration:

Exercise		Set 1	Set 2	Set 3	Set 4	Set 5
	Weight					
	Reps					
	Weight					
	Reps					
	Weight					
	Reps					
	Weight					
	Reps					
	Weight					
	Reps					
	Weight					
	Reps					
	Weight					
	Reps					
	Weight					
	Reps					
	Weight					
	Reps					
	Weight					
	Reps					
	Weight					
	Reps					
	Weight					
	Reps					
	Weight					
	Reps					

CARDIO WORKOUT

Exercise	Duration	Pace	Heart Rate	Calories

WATER 1 cup per circle
(1 cup = 8 ounces ~ 240ml)   ○○○○○○○○○○○○○○○○

DATE:	WEEK:	WEIGHT:

Warm Up/ Stretching		Duration:

Exercise		Set 1	Set 2	Set 3	Set 4	Set 5
	Weight					
	Reps					
	Weight					
	Reps					
	Weight					
	Reps					
	Weight					
	Reps					
	Weight					
	Reps					
	Weight					
	Reps					
	Weight					
	Reps					
	Weight					
	Reps					
	Weight					
	Reps					
	Weight					
	Reps					
	Weight					
	Reps					
	Weight					
	Reps					
	Weight					
	Reps					

CARDIO WORKOUT

Exercise	Duration	Pace	Heart Rate	Calories

WATER 1 cup per circle
(1 cup = 8 ounces ~ 240ml)   ○○○○○○○○○○○○○○○○

DATE: □ WEEK: □ WEIGHT: □

Warm Up/ Stretching

Duration: □

Exercise		Set 1	Set 2	Set 3	Set 4	Set 5
	Weight					
	Reps					
	Weight					
	Reps					
	Weight					
	Reps					
	Weight					
	Reps					
	Weight					
	Reps					
	Weight					
	Reps					
	Weight					
	Reps					
	Weight					
	Reps					
	Weight					
	Reps					
	Weight					
	Reps					
	Weight					
	Reps					
	Weight					
	Reps					
	Weight					
	Reps					

CARDIO WORKOUT

Exercise	Duration	Pace	Heart Rate	Calories

WATER 1 cup per circle
(1 cup = 8 ounces ~ 240ml)

○○○○○○○○○○○○○○○○

DATE:		WEEK:		WEIGHT:	

Warm Up/ Stretching				Duration:	

Exercise		Set 1	Set 2	Set 3	Set 4	Set 5
	Weight					
	Reps					
	Weight					
	Reps					
	Weight					
	Reps					
	Weight					
	Reps					
	Weight					
	Reps					
	Weight					
	Reps					
	Weight					
	Reps					
	Weight					
	Reps					
	Weight					
	Reps					
	Weight					
	Reps					
	Weight					
	Reps					
	Weight					
	Reps					

CARDIO WORKOUT

Exercise	Duration	Pace	Heart Rate	Calories

WATER 1 cup per circle
(1 cup = 8 ounces ~ 240ml)   ○○○○○○○○○○○○○○○

| DATE: | WEEK: | WEIGHT: |

| Warm Up/ Stretching | | | | | Duration: | |

Exercise		Set 1	Set 2	Set 3	Set 4	Set 5
	Weight					
	Reps					
	Weight					
	Reps					
	Weight					
	Reps					
	Weight					
	Reps					
	Weight					
	Reps					
	Weight					
	Reps					
	Weight					
	Reps					
	Weight					
	Reps					
	Weight					
	Reps					
	Weight					
	Reps					
	Weight					
	Reps					
	Weight					
	Reps					

CARDIO WORKOUT

Exercise	Duration	Pace	Heart Rate	Calories

WATER 1 cup per circle
(1 cup = 8 ounces ~ 240ml)   ○○○○○○○○○○○○○○

DATE:	WEEK:	WEIGHT:

Warm Up/ Stretching				Duration:		

Exercise		Set 1	Set 2	Set 3	Set 4	Set 5
	Weight					
	Reps					
	Weight					
	Reps					
	Weight					
	Reps					
	Weight					
	Reps					
	Weight					
	Reps					
	Weight					
	Reps					
	Weight					
	Reps					
	Weight					
	Reps					
	Weight					
	Reps					
	Weight					
	Reps					
	Weight					
	Reps					
	Weight					
	Reps					

CARDIO WORKOUT

Exercise	Duration	Pace	Heart Rate	Calories

WATER 1 cup per circle
(1 cup = 8 ounces ~ 240ml)   ○○○○○○○○○○○○○○○

DATE:	WEEK:	WEIGHT:

Warm Up/ Stretching
Duration:

Exercise		Set 1	Set 2	Set 3	Set 4	Set 5
	Weight					
	Reps					
	Weight					
	Reps					
	Weight					
	Reps					
	Weight					
	Reps					
	Weight					
	Reps					
	Weight					
	Reps					
	Weight					
	Reps					
	Weight					
	Reps					
	Weight					
	Reps					
	Weight					
	Reps					
	Weight					
	Reps					
	Weight					
	Reps					
	Weight					
	Reps					

CARDIO WORKOUT

Exercise	Duration	Pace	Heart Rate	Calories

WATER 1 cup per circle
(1 cup = 8 ounces ~ 240ml)   ○○○○○○○○○○○○○○

DATE: _____ **WEEK:** _____ **WEIGHT:** _____

| Warm Up/ Stretching | | | | | | **Duration:** _____ |

Exercise		Set 1	Set 2	Set 3	Set 4	Set 5
	Weight					
	Reps					
	Weight					
	Reps					
	Weight					
	Reps					
	Weight					
	Reps					
	Weight					
	Reps					
	Weight					
	Reps					
	Weight					
	Reps					
	Weight					
	Reps					
	Weight					
	Reps					
	Weight					
	Reps					
	Weight					
	Reps					
	Weight					
	Reps					

CARDIO WORKOUT

Exercise	Duration	Pace	Heart Rate	Calories

WATER 1 cup per circle
(1 cup = 8 ounces ~ 240ml)   ○○○○○○○○○○○○○○○

DATE: **WEEK:** **WEIGHT:**

Warm Up/ Stretching
Duration:

Exercise		Set 1	Set 2	Set 3	Set 4	Set 5
	Weight					
	Reps					
	Weight					
	Reps					
	Weight					
	Reps					
	Weight					
	Reps					
	Weight					
	Reps					
	Weight					
	Reps					
	Weight					
	Reps					
	Weight					
	Reps					
	Weight					
	Reps					
	Weight					
	Reps					
	Weight					
	Reps					
	Weight					
	Reps					
	Weight					
	Reps					

CARDIO WORKOUT

Exercise	Duration	Pace	Heart Rate	Calories

WATER 1 cup per circle
(1 cup = 8 ounces ~ 240ml)

○ ○ ○ ○ ○ ○ ○ ○ ○ ○ ○ ○

| DATE: | | WEEK: | | WEIGHT: | |

| Warm Up/ Stretching | | | | | Duration: | |

Exercise		Set 1	Set 2	Set 3	Set 4	Set 5
	Weight					
	Reps					
	Weight					
	Reps					
	Weight					
	Reps					
	Weight					
	Reps					
	Weight					
	Reps					
	Weight					
	Reps					
	Weight					
	Reps					
	Weight					
	Reps					
	Weight					
	Reps					
	Weight					
	Reps					
	Weight					
	Reps					
	Weight					
	Reps					
	Weight					
	Reps					

CARDIO WORKOUT

Exercise	Duration	Pace	Heart Rate	Calories

WATER 1 cup per circle
(1 cup = 8 ounces ~ 240ml)   ○○○○○○○○○○○○○○

DATE: | WEEK: | WEIGHT:

Warm Up/ Stretching

Duration:

Exercise		Set 1	Set 2	Set 3	Set 4	Set 5
	Weight					
	Reps					
	Weight					
	Reps					
	Weight					
	Reps					
	Weight					
	Reps					
	Weight					
	Reps					
	Weight					
	Reps					
	Weight					
	Reps					
	Weight					
	Reps					
	Weight					
	Reps					
	Weight					
	Reps					
	Weight					
	Reps					
	Weight					
	Reps					

CARDIO WORKOUT

Exercise	Duration	Pace	Heart Rate	Calories

WATER 1 cup per circle
(1 cup = 8 ounces ~ 240ml)

○○○○○○○○○○○○○○

DATE:		WEEK:		WEIGHT:	

Warm Up/ Stretching
Duration:

Exercise		Set 1	Set 2	Set 3	Set 4	Set 5
	Weight					
	Reps					
	Weight					
	Reps					
	Weight					
	Reps					
	Weight					
	Reps					
	Weight					
	Reps					
	Weight					
	Reps					
	Weight					
	Reps					
	Weight					
	Reps					
	Weight					
	Reps					
	Weight					
	Reps					
	Weight					
	Reps					
	Weight					
	Reps					
	Weight					
	Reps					

CARDIO WORKOUT

Exercise	Duration	Pace	Heart Rate	Calories

WATER 1 cup per circle
(1 cup = 8 ounces ~ 240ml)   ○○○○○○○○○○○○○○○

| DATE: | WEEK: | WEIGHT: |

| Warm Up/ Stretching | | | | Duration: | |

Exercise		Set 1	Set 2	Set 3	Set 4	Set 5
	Weight					
	Reps					
	Weight					
	Reps					
	Weight					
	Reps					
	Weight					
	Reps					
	Weight					
	Reps					
	Weight					
	Reps					
	Weight					
	Reps					
	Weight					
	Reps					
	Weight					
	Reps					
	Weight					
	Reps					
	Weight					
	Reps					
	Weight					
	Reps					
	Weight					
	Reps					

CARDIO WORKOUT

Exercise	Duration	Pace	Heart Rate	Calories

WATER 1 cup per circle
(1 cup = 8 ounces ~ 240ml)   ○○○○○○○○○○○○○○

DATE:		WEEK:		WEIGHT:	

Warm Up/ Stretching				Duration:	

Exercise		Set 1	Set 2	Set 3	Set 4	Set 5
	Weight					
	Reps					
	Weight					
	Reps					
	Weight					
	Reps					
	Weight					
	Reps					
	Weight					
	Reps					
	Weight					
	Reps					
	Weight					
	Reps					
	Weight					
	Reps					
	Weight					
	Reps					
	Weight					
	Reps					
	Weight					
	Reps					
	Weight					
	Reps					
	Weight					
	Reps					

CARDIO WORKOUT

Exercise	Duration	Pace	Heart Rate	Calories

WATER 1 cup per circle
(1 cup = 8 ounces ~ 240ml)   ◯◯◯◯◯◯◯◯◯◯◯◯◯◯

DATE:	WEEK:	WEIGHT:

Warm Up/ Stretching

Duration:

Exercise		Set 1	Set 2	Set 3	Set 4	Set 5
	Weight					
	Reps					
	Weight					
	Reps					
	Weight					
	Reps					
	Weight					
	Reps					
	Weight					
	Reps					
	Weight					
	Reps					
	Weight					
	Reps					
	Weight					
	Reps					
	Weight					
	Reps					
	Weight					
	Reps					
	Weight					
	Reps					
	Weight					
	Reps					
	Weight					
	Reps					

CARDIO WORKOUT

Exercise	Duration	Pace	Heart Rate	Calories

WATER   1 cup per circle
(1 cup = 8 ounces ~ 240ml)

○ ○ ○ ○ ○ ○ ○ ○ ○ ○ ○ ○ ○ ○

DATE:	WEEK:	WEIGHT:

Warm Up/ Stretching		Duration:

Exercise		Set 1	Set 2	Set 3	Set 4	Set 5
	Weight					
	Reps					
	Weight					
	Reps					
	Weight					
	Reps					
	Weight					
	Reps					
	Weight					
	Reps					
	Weight					
	Reps					
	Weight					
	Reps					
	Weight					
	Reps					
	Weight					
	Reps					
	Weight					
	Reps					
	Weight					
	Reps					
	Weight					
	Reps					

CARDIO WORKOUT

Exercise	Duration	Pace	Heart Rate	Calories

WATER 1 cup per circle
(1 cup = 8 ounces ~ 240ml)   ○○○○○○○○○○○○○○○

DATE:	WEEK:	WEIGHT:

Warm Up/ Stretching		Duration:

Exercise		Set 1	Set 2	Set 3	Set 4	Set 5
	Weight					
	Reps					
	Weight					
	Reps					
	Weight					
	Reps					
	Weight					
	Reps					
	Weight					
	Reps					
	Weight					
	Reps					
	Weight					
	Reps					
	Weight					
	Reps					
	Weight					
	Reps					
	Weight					
	Reps					
	Weight					
	Reps					
	Weight					
	Reps					
	Weight					
	Reps					

CARDIO WORKOUT

Exercise	Duration	Pace	Heart Rate	Calories

WATER   1 cup per circle
(1 cup = 8 ounces ~ 240ml)   ○○○○○○○○○○○○○○

DATE:	WEEK:	WEIGHT:

Warm Up/ Stretching

Duration:

Exercise		Set 1	Set 2	Set 3	Set 4	Set 5
	Weight					
	Reps					
	Weight					
	Reps					
	Weight					
	Reps					
	Weight					
	Reps					
	Weight					
	Reps					
	Weight					
	Reps					
	Weight					
	Reps					
	Weight					
	Reps					
	Weight					
	Reps					
	Weight					
	Reps					
	Weight					
	Reps					
	Weight					
	Reps					

CARDIO WORKOUT

Exercise	Duration	Pace	Heart Rate	Calories

WATER 1 cup per circle
(1 cup = 8 ounces ~ 240ml)

○○○○○○○○○○○○○○○

DATE:	WEEK:	WEIGHT:

Warm Up/ Stretching   **Duration:**

Exercise		Set 1	Set 2	Set 3	Set 4	Set 5
	Weight					
	Reps					
	Weight					
	Reps					
	Weight					
	Reps					
	Weight					
	Reps					
	Weight					
	Reps					
	Weight					
	Reps					
	Weight					
	Reps					
	Weight					
	Reps					
	Weight					
	Reps					
	Weight					
	Reps					
	Weight					
	Reps					
	Weight					
	Reps					

CARDIO WORKOUT

Exercise	Duration	Pace	Heart Rate	Calories

WATER   1 cup per circle
(1 cup = 8 ounces ~ 240ml)

○○○○○○○○○○○○○○○

DATE:	WEEK:	WEIGHT:

Warm Up/ Stretching   Duration:

Exercise		Set 1	Set 2	Set 3	Set 4	Set 5
	Weight					
	Reps					
	Weight					
	Reps					
	Weight					
	Reps					
	Weight					
	Reps					
	Weight					
	Reps					
	Weight					
	Reps					
	Weight					
	Reps					
	Weight					
	Reps					
	Weight					
	Reps					
	Weight					
	Reps					
	Weight					
	Reps					
	Weight					
	Reps					

CARDIO WORKOUT

Exercise	Duration	Pace	Heart Rate	Calories

WATER 1 cup per circle
(1 cup = 8 ounces ~ 240ml)   ○○○○○○○○○○○○○○○

| DATE: | WEEK: | WEIGHT: |

| Warm Up/ Stretching | | | | Duration: | |

Exercise		Set 1	Set 2	Set 3	Set 4	Set 5
	Weight					
	Reps					
	Weight					
	Reps					
	Weight					
	Reps					
	Weight					
	Reps					
	Weight					
	Reps					
	Weight					
	Reps					
	Weight					
	Reps					
	Weight					
	Reps					
	Weight					
	Reps					
	Weight					
	Reps					
	Weight					
	Reps					
	Weight					
	Reps					

CARDIO WORKOUT

Exercise	Duration	Pace	Heart Rate	Calories

WATER 1 cup per circle
(1 cup = 8 ounces ~ 240ml)   ○○○○○○○○○○○○

DATE:		WEEK:		WEIGHT:	

Warm Up/ Stretching				Duration:	

Exercise		Set 1	Set 2	Set 3	Set 4	Set 5
	Weight					
	Reps					
	Weight					
	Reps					
	Weight					
	Reps					
	Weight					
	Reps					
	Weight					
	Reps					
	Weight					
	Reps					
	Weight					
	Reps					
	Weight					
	Reps					
	Weight					
	Reps					
	Weight					
	Reps					
	Weight					
	Reps					
	Weight					
	Reps					

CARDIO WORKOUT

Exercise	Duration	Pace	Heart Rate	Calories

WATER 1 cup per circle
(1 cup = 8 ounces ~ 240ml)   ○○○○○○○○○○○○○○○○

| DATE: | | WEEK: | | WEIGHT: | |

| Warm Up/ Stretching | | | | Duration: | |

Exercise		Set 1	Set 2	Set 3	Set 4	Set 5
	Weight					
	Reps					
	Weight					
	Reps					
	Weight					
	Reps					
	Weight					
	Reps					
	Weight					
	Reps					
	Weight					
	Reps					
	Weight					
	Reps					
	Weight					
	Reps					
	Weight					
	Reps					
	Weight					
	Reps					
	Weight					
	Reps					
	Weight					
	Reps					
	Weight					
	Reps					

CARDIO WORKOUT

Exercise	Duration	Pace	Heart Rate	Calories

WATER 1 cup per circle
(1 cup = 8 ounces ~ 240ml)   ○○○○○○○○○○○○○○○○

DATE:	WEEK:	WEIGHT:

Warm Up/ Stretching		Duration:

Exercise		Set 1	Set 2	Set 3	Set 4	Set 5
	Weight					
	Reps					
	Weight					
	Reps					
	Weight					
	Reps					
	Weight					
	Reps					
	Weight					
	Reps					
	Weight					
	Reps					
	Weight					
	Reps					
	Weight					
	Reps					
	Weight					
	Reps					
	Weight					
	Reps					
	Weight					
	Reps					
	Weight					
	Reps					

CARDIO WORKOUT

Exercise	Duration	Pace	Heart Rate	Calories

WATER 1 cup per circle
(1 cup = 8 ounces ~ 240ml)   ○○○○○○○○○○○○○○○

DATE:	WEEK:	WEIGHT:

Warm Up/ Stretching

Duration:

Exercise		Set 1	Set 2	Set 3	Set 4	Set 5
	Weight					
	Reps					
	Weight					
	Reps					
	Weight					
	Reps					
	Weight					
	Reps					
	Weight					
	Reps					
	Weight					
	Reps					
	Weight					
	Reps					
	Weight					
	Reps					
	Weight					
	Reps					
	Weight					
	Reps					
	Weight					
	Reps					
	Weight					
	Reps					

CARDIO WORKOUT

Exercise	Duration	Pace	Heart Rate	Calories

WATER   1 cup per circle
(1 cup = 8 ounces ~ 240ml)

○○○○○○○○○○○○○○○○

DATE:		WEEK:		WEIGHT:	

Warm Up/ Stretching				Duration:	

Exercise		Set 1	Set 2	Set 3	Set 4	Set 5
	Weight					
	Reps					
	Weight					
	Reps					
	Weight					
	Reps					
	Weight					
	Reps					
	Weight					
	Reps					
	Weight					
	Reps					
	Weight					
	Reps					
	Weight					
	Reps					
	Weight					
	Reps					
	Weight					
	Reps					
	Weight					
	Reps					
	Weight					
	Reps					
	Weight					
	Reps					

CARDIO WORKOUT

Exercise	Duration	Pace	Heart Rate	Calories

WATER 1 cup per circle
(1 cup = 8 ounces ~ 240ml) ○○○○○○○○○○○○○○○

DATE: _____ WEEK: _____ WEIGHT: _____

Warm Up/ Stretching   Duration: _____

Exercise		Set 1	Set 2	Set 3	Set 4	Set 5
	Weight					
	Reps					
	Weight					
	Reps					
	Weight					
	Reps					
	Weight					
	Reps					
	Weight					
	Reps					
	Weight					
	Reps					
	Weight					
	Reps					
	Weight					
	Reps					
	Weight					
	Reps					
	Weight					
	Reps					
	Weight					
	Reps					
	Weight					
	Reps					
	Weight					
	Reps					

CARDIO WORKOUT

Exercise	Duration	Pace	Heart Rate	Calories

WATER 1 cup per circle
(1 cup = 8 ounces ~ 240ml)   ◯◯◯◯◯◯◯◯◯◯◯◯◯

DATE:		WEEK:		WEIGHT:	

Warm Up/ Stretching	Duration:

Exercise		Set 1	Set 2	Set 3	Set 4	Set 5
	Weight					
	Reps					
	Weight					
	Reps					
	Weight					
	Reps					
	Weight					
	Reps					
	Weight					
	Reps					
	Weight					
	Reps					
	Weight					
	Reps					
	Weight					
	Reps					
	Weight					
	Reps					
	Weight					
	Reps					
	Weight					
	Reps					
	Weight					
	Reps					

CARDIO WORKOUT

Exercise	Duration	Pace	Heart Rate	Calories

WATER 1 cup per circle
(1 cup = 8 ounces ~ 240ml)   ○○○○○○○○○○○○○○○

DATE:		WEEK:		WEIGHT:	

Warm Up/ Stretching
Duration:

Exercise		Set 1	Set 2	Set 3	Set 4	Set 5
	Weight					
	Reps					
	Weight					
	Reps					
	Weight					
	Reps					
	Weight					
	Reps					
	Weight					
	Reps					
	Weight					
	Reps					
	Weight					
	Reps					
	Weight					
	Reps					
	Weight					
	Reps					
	Weight					
	Reps					
	Weight					
	Reps					
	Weight					
	Reps					

CARDIO WORKOUT

Exercise	Duration	Pace	Heart Rate	Calories

WATER   1 cup per circle
(1 cup = 8 ounces ~ 240ml)

○ ○ ○ ○ ○ ○ ○ ○ ○ ○ ○ ○ ○ ○

DATE: **WEEK:** **WEIGHT:**

Warm Up/ Stretching **Duration:**

Exercise		Set 1	Set 2	Set 3	Set 4	Set 5
	Weight					
	Reps					
	Weight					
	Reps					
	Weight					
	Reps					
	Weight					
	Reps					
	Weight					
	Reps					
	Weight					
	Reps					
	Weight					
	Reps					
	Weight					
	Reps					
	Weight					
	Reps					
	Weight					
	Reps					
	Weight					
	Reps					
	Weight					
	Reps					

CARDIO WORKOUT

Exercise	Duration	Pace	Heart Rate	Calories

WATER 1 cup per circle
(1 cup = 8 ounces ~ 240ml)

○○○○○○○○○○○○○○○○

DATE: _____ WEEK: _____ WEIGHT: _____

Warm Up/ Stretching

Duration: _____

Exercise		Set 1	Set 2	Set 3	Set 4	Set 5
	Weight					
	Reps					
	Weight					
	Reps					
	Weight					
	Reps					
	Weight					
	Reps					
	Weight					
	Reps					
	Weight					
	Reps					
	Weight					
	Reps					
	Weight					
	Reps					
	Weight					
	Reps					
	Weight					
	Reps					
	Weight					
	Reps					
	Weight					
	Reps					
	Weight					
	Reps					

CARDIO WORKOUT

Exercise	Duration	Pace	Heart Rate	Calories

WATER 1 cup per circle
(1 cup = 8 ounces ~ 240ml)   ○○○○○○○○○○○○○○

DATE:	WEEK:	WEIGHT:

Warm Up/ Stretching		Duration:

Exercise		Set 1	Set 2	Set 3	Set 4	Set 5
	Weight					
	Reps					
	Weight					
	Reps					
	Weight					
	Reps					
	Weight					
	Reps					
	Weight					
	Reps					
	Weight					
	Reps					
	Weight					
	Reps					
	Weight					
	Reps					
	Weight					
	Reps					
	Weight					
	Reps					
	Weight					
	Reps					
	Weight					
	Reps					
	Weight					
	Reps					

CARDIO WORKOUT

Exercise	Duration	Pace	Heart Rate	Calories

WATER 1 cup per circle
(1 cup = 8 ounces ~ 240ml)

○○○○○○○○○○○○○○○○

DATE:	WEEK:	WEIGHT:

Warm Up/ Stretching — Duration:

Exercise		Set 1	Set 2	Set 3	Set 4	Set 5
	Weight					
	Reps					
	Weight					
	Reps					
	Weight					
	Reps					
	Weight					
	Reps					
	Weight					
	Reps					
	Weight					
	Reps					
	Weight					
	Reps					
	Weight					
	Reps					
	Weight					
	Reps					
	Weight					
	Reps					
	Weight					
	Reps					
	Weight					
	Reps					

CARDIO WORKOUT

Exercise	Duration	Pace	Heart Rate	Calories

WATER 1 cup per circle
(1 cup = 8 ounces ~ 240ml)

○○○○○○○○○○○○○○

DATE:		WEEK:		WEIGHT:	

Warm Up/ Stretching				Duration:	

Exercise		Set 1	Set 2	Set 3	Set 4	Set 5
	Weight					
	Reps					
	Weight					
	Reps					
	Weight					
	Reps					
	Weight					
	Reps					
	Weight					
	Reps					
	Weight					
	Reps					
	Weight					
	Reps					
	Weight					
	Reps					
	Weight					
	Reps					
	Weight					
	Reps					
	Weight					
	Reps					
	Weight					
	Reps					
	Weight					
	Reps					

CARDIO WORKOUT

Exercise	Duration	Pace	Heart Rate	Calories

WATER 1 cup per circle
(1 cup = 8 ounces ~ 240ml)

○○○○○○○○○○○○○○○

DATE:	WEEK:	WEIGHT:

Warm Up/ Stretching
Duration:

Exercise		Set 1	Set 2	Set 3	Set 4	Set 5
	Weight					
	Reps					
	Weight					
	Reps					
	Weight					
	Reps					
	Weight					
	Reps					
	Weight					
	Reps					
	Weight					
	Reps					
	Weight					
	Reps					
	Weight					
	Reps					
	Weight					
	Reps					
	Weight					
	Reps					
	Weight					
	Reps					
	Weight					
	Reps					

CARDIO WORKOUT

Exercise	Duration	Pace	Heart Rate	Calories

WATER 1 cup per circle
(1 cup = 8 ounces ~ 240ml)

○ ○ ○ ○ ○ ○ ○ ○ ○ ○ ○ ○ ○ ○ ○

DATE:		WEEK:		WEIGHT:	

Warm Up/ Stretching			Duration:	

Exercise		Set 1	Set 2	Set 3	Set 4	Set 5
	Weight					
	Reps					
	Weight					
	Reps					
	Weight					
	Reps					
	Weight					
	Reps					
	Weight					
	Reps					
	Weight					
	Reps					
	Weight					
	Reps					
	Weight					
	Reps					
	Weight					
	Reps					
	Weight					
	Reps					
	Weight					
	Reps					
	Weight					
	Reps					
	Weight					
	Reps					

CARDIO WORKOUT

Exercise	Duration	Pace	Heart Rate	Calories

WATER 1 cup per circle
(1 cup = 8 ounces ~ 240ml)   ○○○○○○○○○○○○○○○○

DATE:	WEEK:	WEIGHT:

Warm Up/ Stretching
Duration:

Exercise		Set 1	Set 2	Set 3	Set 4	Set 5
	Weight					
	Reps					
	Weight					
	Reps					
	Weight					
	Reps					
	Weight					
	Reps					
	Weight					
	Reps					
	Weight					
	Reps					
	Weight					
	Reps					
	Weight					
	Reps					
	Weight					
	Reps					
	Weight					
	Reps					
	Weight					
	Reps					
	Weight					
	Reps					
	Weight					
	Reps					

CARDIO WORKOUT

Exercise	Duration	Pace	Heart Rate	Calories

WATER 1 cup per circle
(1 cup = 8 ounces ~ 240ml)   ○ ○ ○ ○ ○ ○ ○ ○ ○ ○ ○ ○

DATE:		WEEK:		WEIGHT:	

Warm Up/ Stretching				Duration:	

Exercise		Set 1	Set 2	Set 3	Set 4	Set 5
	Weight					
	Reps					
	Weight					
	Reps					
	Weight					
	Reps					
	Weight					
	Reps					
	Weight					
	Reps					
	Weight					
	Reps					
	Weight					
	Reps					
	Weight					
	Reps					
	Weight					
	Reps					
	Weight					
	Reps					
	Weight					
	Reps					
	Weight					
	Reps					

CARDIO WORKOUT

Exercise	Duration	Pace	Heart Rate	Calories

WATER 1 cup per circle
(1 cup = 8 ounces ~ 240ml)   ○○○○○○○○○○○○○○○

DATE:	WEEK:	WEIGHT:

Warm Up/ Stretching		Duration:	

Exercise		Set 1	Set 2	Set 3	Set 4	Set 5
	Weight					
	Reps					
	Weight					
	Reps					
	Weight					
	Reps					
	Weight					
	Reps					
	Weight					
	Reps					
	Weight					
	Reps					
	Weight					
	Reps					
	Weight					
	Reps					
	Weight					
	Reps					
	Weight					
	Reps					
	Weight					
	Reps					
	Weight					
	Reps					
	Weight					
	Reps					

CARDIO WORKOUT

Exercise	Duration	Pace	Heart Rate	Calories

WATER 1 cup per circle
(1 cup = 8 ounces ~ 240ml)

○ ○ ○ ○ ○ ○ ○ ○ ○ ○ ○ ○

DATE: _____ **WEEK:** _____ **WEIGHT:** _____

Warm Up/ Stretching				**Duration:**	

Exercise		Set 1	Set 2	Set 3	Set 4	Set 5
	Weight					
	Reps					
	Weight					
	Reps					
	Weight					
	Reps					
	Weight					
	Reps					
	Weight					
	Reps					
	Weight					
	Reps					
	Weight					
	Reps					
	Weight					
	Reps					
	Weight					
	Reps					
	Weight					
	Reps					
	Weight					
	Reps					
	Weight					
	Reps					
	Weight					
	Reps					

CARDIO WORKOUT

Exercise	Duration	Pace	Heart Rate	Calories

WATER   1 cup per circle
(1 cup = 8 ounces ~ 240ml)   ○○○○○○○○○○○○○○○○

DATE: **WEEK:**   **WEIGHT:**

Warm Up/ Stretching   **Duration:**

Exercise		Set 1	Set 2	Set 3	Set 4	Set 5
	Weight					
	Reps					
	Weight					
	Reps					
	Weight					
	Reps					
	Weight					
	Reps					
	Weight					
	Reps					
	Weight					
	Reps					
	Weight					
	Reps					
	Weight					
	Reps					
	Weight					
	Reps					
	Weight					
	Reps					
	Weight					
	Reps					
	Weight					
	Reps					
	Weight					
	Reps					

CARDIO WORKOUT

Exercise	Duration	Pace	Heart Rate	Calories

WATER   1 cup per circle
(1 cup = 8 ounces ~ 240ml)   ○ ○ ○ ○ ○ ○ ○ ○ ○ ○ ○ ○ ○ ○ ○

DATE:	WEEK:	WEIGHT:

Warm Up/ Stretching	Duration:

Exercise		Set 1	Set 2	Set 3	Set 4	Set 5
	Weight					
	Reps					
	Weight					
	Reps					
	Weight					
	Reps					
	Weight					
	Reps					
	Weight					
	Reps					
	Weight					
	Reps					
	Weight					
	Reps					
	Weight					
	Reps					
	Weight					
	Reps					
	Weight					
	Reps					
	Weight					
	Reps					
	Weight					
	Reps					

CARDIO WORKOUT

Exercise	Duration	Pace	Heart Rate	Calories

WATER 1 cup per circle
(1 cup = 8 ounces ~ 240ml)

○○○○○○○○○○○○○○○○○

DATE:	WEEK:	WEIGHT:

Warm Up/ Stretching

Duration:

Exercise		Set 1	Set 2	Set 3	Set 4	Set 5
	Weight					
	Reps					
	Weight					
	Reps					
	Weight					
	Reps					
	Weight					
	Reps					
	Weight					
	Reps					
	Weight					
	Reps					
	Weight					
	Reps					
	Weight					
	Reps					
	Weight					
	Reps					
	Weight					
	Reps					
	Weight					
	Reps					
	Weight					
	Reps					
	Weight					
	Reps					

CARDIO WORKOUT

Exercise	Duration	Pace	Heart Rate	Calories

WATER 1 cup per circle
(1 cup = 8 ounces ~ 240ml)

○ ○ ○ ○ ○ ○ ○ ○ ○ ○ ○ ○

DATE:	WEEK:	WEIGHT:

Warm Up/ Stretching — Duration:

Exercise		Set 1	Set 2	Set 3	Set 4	Set 5
	Weight					
	Reps					
	Weight					
	Reps					
	Weight					
	Reps					
	Weight					
	Reps					
	Weight					
	Reps					
	Weight					
	Reps					
	Weight					
	Reps					
	Weight					
	Reps					
	Weight					
	Reps					
	Weight					
	Reps					
	Weight					
	Reps					
	Weight					
	Reps					

CARDIO WORKOUT

Exercise	Duration	Pace	Heart Rate	Calories

WATER 1 cup per circle
(1 cup = 8 ounces ~ 240ml)

○○○○○○○○○○○○○○○

DATE:	WEEK:	WEIGHT:

Warm Up/ Stretching
Duration:

Exercise		Set 1	Set 2	Set 3	Set 4	Set 5
	Weight					
	Reps					
	Weight					
	Reps					
	Weight					
	Reps					
	Weight					
	Reps					
	Weight					
	Reps					
	Weight					
	Reps					
	Weight					
	Reps					
	Weight					
	Reps					
	Weight					
	Reps					
	Weight					
	Reps					
	Weight					
	Reps					
	Weight					
	Reps					
	Weight					
	Reps					

CARDIO WORKOUT

Exercise	Duration	Pace	Heart Rate	Calories

WATER 1 cup per circle
(1 cup = 8 ounces ~ 240ml)   ○○○○○○○○○○○○○○

| DATE: | | WEEK: | | WEIGHT: | |

| Warm Up/ Stretching | | | | Duration: | |

Exercise		Set 1	Set 2	Set 3	Set 4	Set 5
	Weight					
	Reps					
	Weight					
	Reps					
	Weight					
	Reps					
	Weight					
	Reps					
	Weight					
	Reps					
	Weight					
	Reps					
	Weight					
	Reps					
	Weight					
	Reps					
	Weight					
	Reps					
	Weight					
	Reps					
	Weight					
	Reps					
	Weight					
	Reps					
	Weight					
	Reps					

CARDIO WORKOUT

Exercise	Duration	Pace	Heart Rate	Calories

WATER 1 cup per circle
(1 cup = 8 ounces ~ 240ml)

○○○○○○○○○○○○○○○○

DATE:	WEEK:	WEIGHT:

Warm Up/ Stretching
Duration:

Exercise		Set 1	Set 2	Set 3	Set 4	Set 5
	Weight					
	Reps					
	Weight					
	Reps					
	Weight					
	Reps					
	Weight					
	Reps					
	Weight					
	Reps					
	Weight					
	Reps					
	Weight					
	Reps					
	Weight					
	Reps					
	Weight					
	Reps					
	Weight					
	Reps					
	Weight					
	Reps					
	Weight					
	Reps					
	Weight					
	Reps					

CARDIO WORKOUT

Exercise	Duration	Pace	Heart Rate	Calories

WATER 1 cup per circle
(1 cup = 8 ounces ~ 240ml)

○○○○○○○○○○○○○○○

DATE:		WEEK:		WEIGHT:	

Warm Up/ Stretching				Duration:	

Exercise		Set 1	Set 2	Set 3	Set 4	Set 5
	Weight					
	Reps					
	Weight					
	Reps					
	Weight					
	Reps					
	Weight					
	Reps					
	Weight					
	Reps					
	Weight					
	Reps					
	Weight					
	Reps					
	Weight					
	Reps					
	Weight					
	Reps					
	Weight					
	Reps					
	Weight					
	Reps					
	Weight					
	Reps					
	Weight					
	Reps					

CARDIO WORKOUT

Exercise	Duration	Pace	Heart Rate	Calories

WATER 1 cup per circle
(1 cup = 8 ounces ~ 240ml)

○○○○○○○○○○○○○○○

DATE:	WEEK:	WEIGHT:

Warm Up/ Stretching		Duration:				
Exercise		Set 1	Set 2	Set 3	Set 4	Set 5
	Weight					
	Reps					
	Weight					
	Reps					
	Weight					
	Reps					
	Weight					
	Reps					
	Weight					
	Reps					
	Weight					
	Reps					
	Weight					
	Reps					
	Weight					
	Reps					
	Weight					
	Reps					
	Weight					
	Reps					
	Weight					
	Reps					
	Weight					
	Reps					
	Weight					
	Reps					

CARDIO WORKOUT

Exercise	Duration	Pace	Heart Rate	Calories

WATER 1 cup per circle
(1 cup = 8 ounces ~ 240ml)   ○○○○○○○○○○○○○○○○

DATE: [ ] WEEK: [ ] WEIGHT: [ ]

Warm Up/ Stretching   Duration: [ ]

Exercise		Set 1	Set 2	Set 3	Set 4	Set 5
	Weight					
	Reps					
	Weight					
	Reps					
	Weight					
	Reps					
	Weight					
	Reps					
	Weight					
	Reps					
	Weight					
	Reps					
	Weight					
	Reps					
	Weight					
	Reps					
	Weight					
	Reps					
	Weight					
	Reps					
	Weight					
	Reps					
	Weight					
	Reps					
	Weight					
	Reps					

CARDIO WORKOUT

Exercise	Duration	Pace	Heart Rate	Calories

WATER 1 cup per circle
(1 cup = 8 ounces ~ 240ml)   ○○○○○○○○○○○○○○○

DATE:	WEEK:	WEIGHT:

Warm Up/ Stretching

Duration:

Exercise		Set 1	Set 2	Set 3	Set 4	Set 5
	Weight					
	Reps					
	Weight					
	Reps					
	Weight					
	Reps					
	Weight					
	Reps					
	Weight					
	Reps					
	Weight					
	Reps					
	Weight					
	Reps					
	Weight					
	Reps					
	Weight					
	Reps					
	Weight					
	Reps					
	Weight					
	Reps					
	Weight					
	Reps					

CARDIO WORKOUT

Exercise	Duration	Pace	Heart Rate	Calories

WATER 1 cup per circle
(1 cup = 8 ounces ~ 240ml)

○○○○○○○○○○○○○○○○

DATE:	WEEK:	WEIGHT:

Warm Up/ Stretching   Duration:

Exercise		Set 1	Set 2	Set 3	Set 4	Set 5
	Weight					
	Reps					
	Weight					
	Reps					
	Weight					
	Reps					
	Weight					
	Reps					
	Weight					
	Reps					
	Weight					
	Reps					
	Weight					
	Reps					
	Weight					
	Reps					
	Weight					
	Reps					
	Weight					
	Reps					
	Weight					
	Reps					
	Weight					
	Reps					

CARDIO WORKOUT

Exercise	Duration	Pace	Heart Rate	Calories

WATER 1 cup per circle
(1 cup = 8 ounces ~ 240ml)

○○○○○○○○○○○○○○○○

| DATE: | | WEEK: | | WEIGHT: | |

Warm Up/ Stretching

Duration:

Exercise		Set 1	Set 2	Set 3	Set 4	Set 5
	Weight					
	Reps					
	Weight					
	Reps					
	Weight					
	Reps					
	Weight					
	Reps					
	Weight					
	Reps					
	Weight					
	Reps					
	Weight					
	Reps					
	Weight					
	Reps					
	Weight					
	Reps					
	Weight					
	Reps					
	Weight					
	Reps					
	Weight					
	Reps					

CARDIO WORKOUT

Exercise	Duration	Pace	Heart Rate	Calories

WATER 1 cup per circle
(1 cup = 8 ounces ~ 240ml)

○○○○○○○○○○○○○○○

DATE: ____ WEEK: ____ WEIGHT: ____

Warm Up/ Stretching   Duration: ____

Exercise		Set 1	Set 2	Set 3	Set 4	Set 5
	Weight					
	Reps					
	Weight					
	Reps					
	Weight					
	Reps					
	Weight					
	Reps					
	Weight					
	Reps					
	Weight					
	Reps					
	Weight					
	Reps					
	Weight					
	Reps					
	Weight					
	Reps					
	Weight					
	Reps					
	Weight					
	Reps					
	Weight					
	Reps					

CARDIO WORKOUT

Exercise	Duration	Pace	Heart Rate	Calories

WATER   1 cup per circle
(1 cup = 8 ounces ~ 240ml)   ○○○○○○○○○○○○○○

DATE:		WEEK:		WEIGHT:	

Warm Up/ Stretching				Duration:	

Exercise		Set 1	Set 2	Set 3	Set 4	Set 5
	Weight					
	Reps					
	Weight					
	Reps					
	Weight					
	Reps					
	Weight					
	Reps					
	Weight					
	Reps					
	Weight					
	Reps					
	Weight					
	Reps					
	Weight					
	Reps					
	Weight					
	Reps					
	Weight					
	Reps					
	Weight					
	Reps					
	Weight					
	Reps					
	Weight					
	Reps					

CARDIO WORKOUT

Exercise	Duration	Pace	Heart Rate	Calories

WATER 1 cup per circle
(1 cup = 8 ounces ~ 240ml)

○ ○ ○ ○ ○ ○ ○ ○ ○ ○ ○ ○ ○ ○

DATE:	WEEK:	WEIGHT:

Warm Up/ Stretching

Duration:

Exercise		Set 1	Set 2	Set 3	Set 4	Set 5
	Weight					
	Reps					
	Weight					
	Reps					
	Weight					
	Reps					
	Weight					
	Reps					
	Weight					
	Reps					
	Weight					
	Reps					
	Weight					
	Reps					
	Weight					
	Reps					
	Weight					
	Reps					
	Weight					
	Reps					
	Weight					
	Reps					
	Weight					
	Reps					

CARDIO WORKOUT

Exercise	Duration	Pace	Heart Rate	Calories

WATER 1 cup per circle
(1 cup = 8 ounces ~ 240ml)

○○○○○○○○○○○○○○○○

DATE: _____ WEEK: _____ WEIGHT: _____

Warm Up/ Stretching

Duration: _____

Exercise		Set 1	Set 2	Set 3	Set 4	Set 5
	Weight					
	Reps					
	Weight					
	Reps					
	Weight					
	Reps					
	Weight					
	Reps					
	Weight					
	Reps					
	Weight					
	Reps					
	Weight					
	Reps					
	Weight					
	Reps					
	Weight					
	Reps					
	Weight					
	Reps					
	Weight					
	Reps					
	Weight					
	Reps					

CARDIO WORKOUT

Exercise	Duration	Pace	Heart Rate	Calories

WATER 1 cup per circle
(1 cup = 8 ounces ~ 240ml)

○ ○ ○ ○ ○ ○ ○ ○ ○ ○ ○ ○ ○ ○

DATE:		WEEK:		WEIGHT:	

Warm Up/ Stretching

Duration:

Exercise		Set 1	Set 2	Set 3	Set 4	Set 5
	Weight					
	Reps					
	Weight					
	Reps					
	Weight					
	Reps					
	Weight					
	Reps					
	Weight					
	Reps					
	Weight					
	Reps					
	Weight					
	Reps					
	Weight					
	Reps					
	Weight					
	Reps					
	Weight					
	Reps					
	Weight					
	Reps					
	Weight					
	Reps					

CARDIO WORKOUT

Exercise	Duration	Pace	Heart Rate	Calories

WATER 1 cup per circle
(1 cup = 8 ounces ~ 240ml)

○○○○○○○○○○○○○○○○

DATE:		WEEK:		WEIGHT:	

Warm Up/ Stretching Duration:

Exercise		Set 1	Set 2	Set 3	Set 4	Set 5
	Weight					
	Reps					
	Weight					
	Reps					
	Weight					
	Reps					
	Weight					
	Reps					
	Weight					
	Reps					
	Weight					
	Reps					
	Weight					
	Reps					
	Weight					
	Reps					
	Weight					
	Reps					
	Weight					
	Reps					
	Weight					
	Reps					
	Weight					
	Reps					
	Weight					
	Reps					

CARDIO WORKOUT

Exercise	Duration	Pace	Heart Rate	Calories

WATER 1 cup per circle
(1 cup = 8 ounces ~ 240ml)

○○○○○○○○○○○○○○○○

DATE:		WEEK:		WEIGHT:	

Warm Up/ Stretching				Duration:	

Exercise		Set 1	Set 2	Set 3	Set 4	Set 5
	Weight					
	Reps					
	Weight					
	Reps					
	Weight					
	Reps					
	Weight					
	Reps					
	Weight					
	Reps					
	Weight					
	Reps					
	Weight					
	Reps					
	Weight					
	Reps					
	Weight					
	Reps					
	Weight					
	Reps					
	Weight					
	Reps					
	Weight					
	Reps					

CARDIO WORKOUT

Exercise	Duration	Pace	Heart Rate	Calories

WATER 1 cup per circle
(1 cup = 8 ounces ~ 240ml)   ○○○○○○○○○○○○○○○○

DATE:		WEEK:		WEIGHT:	

Warm Up/ Stretching					Duration:	

Exercise		Set 1	Set 2	Set 3	Set 4	Set 5
	Weight					
	Reps					
	Weight					
	Reps					
	Weight					
	Reps					
	Weight					
	Reps					
	Weight					
	Reps					
	Weight					
	Reps					
	Weight					
	Reps					
	Weight					
	Reps					
	Weight					
	Reps					
	Weight					
	Reps					
	Weight					
	Reps					
	Weight					
	Reps					
	Weight					
	Reps					

CARDIO WORKOUT

Exercise	Duration	Pace	Heart Rate	Calories

WATER 1 cup per circle
(1 cup = 8 ounces ~ 240ml)   ○○○○○○○○○○○○○

Made in the USA
Columbia, SC
15 January 2025